Anna Claybourne • illustrations by Jan Van Der Veken

THE HISTORY OF EVERYTHING

(IN 32 PAGES)

Laurence King Publishing

TIMELINE (OF EVERYTHING)

BANG!!!

13.8–4.6 billion years ago

The Universe unfolds, expanding from a single point in space to form stars and galaxies, including our own Milky Way.

Page 4

OUR HOME IN SPACE

4.6 billion years ago

The Sun and the planets, including our own Earth, are formed and the Solar System takes shape.

Page 6

THE EARLY EARTH

4.5–4 billion years ago

Early Earth evolves from a hot, rocky, uninhabitable planet into somewhere capable of supporting life.

Page 8

LIFE BEGINS

4 billion–500 million years ago

From the very first simple cells to the arrival of fish, early evolution leads to life on Earth.

Page 10

LAND INVASION

500–250 million years ago

Life moves out of the water and takes its first steps on dry land.

Page 12

THE DINOSAUR AGE

250–60 million years ago

Giant reptiles not only roam the earth but also rule the skies and seas.

Page 14

RISE OF THE MAMMALS

60–6 million years ago

Following the extinction of the dinosaurs, plant and animal life recover and mammals begin their takeover.

Page 16

THE FIRST HUMANS

6 million–12 thousand years ago

Our human ancestors evolve alongside other apes, spreading around the globe and establishing new ways of living.

Page 18

SETTLING DOWN

12–6 thousand years ago

People put down roots, building early settlements and beginning to farm crops and breed animals.

Page 20

CITIES, CIVILIZATIONS, AND EMPIRES

4,000 BCE–500 CE

Early societies become more sophisticated, with world-changing inventions and the evolution of powerful global empires.

Page 22

SCIENCE, ART, AND DISCOVERY

500–1600s

An age of exploration and invention, where adventurers travel afar and art and science flourishes around the world.

Page 24

INDUSTRIAL REVOLUTION

1700–1840s

British industrialization rapidly spreads worldwide, changing the way people live forever.

Page 26

TECHNOLOGY

1840s–1940s

Newly revolutionized industry gives rise to a century of innovation, from manned flight to telecommunications and computing.

Page 28

THE MODERN AGE

1940–the present day

Technological innovations shape both the world we live in and the future that we face.

Page 30

In the beginning, about 13.8 billion years ago, the Universe started with a bang. From a single, tiny point, it suddenly expanded into a huge cloud of energy and particles of matter. The Big Bang, as it is called, sounds as though it was an explosion, but it wasn't. It was a very quick, sudden expansion: imagine a balloon popping, but in reverse. It was a bit like that!

The Universe didn't expand into a space that already existed. All of space was held inside that tiny single point. This early expansion, the Big Bang, was the start of space and time.

150 million years:
The universe is made up of dark clouds of gases, mainly helium and hydrogen.

380,000 years:
Atoms start to form, with electrons orbiting around nucleuses.

3 minutes:
The nucleuses of simple, light elements start to form.

One 100-millionth of a second:
Particles of matter form.

0 seconds:
Big Bang (the beginning of time).

Hydrogen atom

Helium nucleus

Hydrogen nucleus

Helium atom

Electrons

Neutrons

Protons

How do we know?

Using telescopes, we can see that stars and galaxies in the Universe are moving apart from one another. Working backward, scientists think that means the Universe must have started expanding long ago, and was once just a single point. We can also detect something called the Cosmic Microwave Background. This is a type of faint energy filling the Universe, left over from the huge release of energy during the Big Bang.

Looking into the past

The Universe is so big that light takes billions of years to travel across it. So, when we use telescopes to look at distant galaxies, we're actually looking back in time, too. The light we see coming from them set off on its journey to our eyes billions of years ago. In 2016 NASA's Hubble Space Telescope looked at the farthest galaxy it had ever seen—named GN-z11, it is 13.4 billion light years from our Earth.

200 million years:
Gradually, gravity pulls clouds of gas together. They form dense spheres of helium and hydrogen: the first stars. The stars glow as the gas molecules inside them fuse together and release energy.

400 million years:
Stars themselves also pull together into groups because of their gravity. They start to form huge clusters called galaxies. Galaxies draw in more dust and gas, and form more stars.

1 billion years:
One of these galaxies starts as a ball-shaped cluster of stars, then spins out to form a wide, flat disc with spiraling arms. It's the galaxy that will become our home, which we now call the Milky Way.

Our galaxy

The Milky Way, our galaxy, is shaped like a disc, about 150,000 light years across. That means it would take a beam of light 150,000 years to travel from one side of it to the other. The thickness of the disc is about 1,000 light years. When we look at the night sky, we are seeing our galaxy from near one edge of the swirling disc shape.

From Earth, we can see the stars in the rest of the galaxy. The thickest part appears as a band of stars across the night sky. Ancient people thought this looked like a road or river of milk, and that led to the name "Milky Way."

Our own home star, the Sun, and the Solar System around it formed much later—about 4.6 billion years ago.

OUR HOME IN SPACE

About 4.6 billion years ago, in one of the Milky Way's spiral arms, a new star began to form. Clouds of gas and dust collapsed together to form a dense, spinning mass. As it rotated, it spread out into a flat disc shape.

In the middle, gases collected to form a hot, glowing star, and in the disc around it, matter began to collide and clump together, creating planets orbiting the star.

We now call this star the Sun. The Sun and the planets and other objects that orbit it are known as the Solar System (from "Sol," the Roman name for the Sun). The Sun is by far the biggest object in the Solar System, at about 870,000 miles across.

Like other stars, the Sun began to glow with light and heat as the gases inside it fused together. This heated up the part of the Solar System nearest the Sun, while the outer Solar System was cooler.

Moons
Most planets have moons, smaller planet-like objects that orbit them. Earth has just one moon, but Jupiter and Saturn have more than 60 moons each.

Rocky planets

Close to the Sun, only elements that were solid or liquid at high temperatures could clump together to make planets. So the planets that formed near the Sun were made of rocky and metallic elements such as iron and silicon. They are the terrestrial planets—Mercury, Venus, Earth, and Mars—and they were formed about 100 million years after the start of the Solar System, much later than the gas giants.

Mercury
The closest planet to the Sun, Mercury is the smallest planet in the Solar System.

Venus
This hot, highly volcanic planet rotates very slowly, so the sun rises on Venus only once every 117 Earth days.

Earth
The watery, medium-warm planet where life, civilization, and history would eventually come into existence.

Mars
Mars is sometimes called the Red Planet, thanks to the color of its rocky surface.

Asteroids
Between Mars and Jupiter, millions of asteroids, small leftover lumps of rock, orbit the Sun in the Asteroid Belt.

The outer reaches

The Sun and the planets are not the whole Solar System. Much further out, millions of dwarf planets orbit the Sun in the Kuiper Belt. Even further away, a vast ball-shaped cloud of icy objects, the Oort Cloud, surrounds the Solar System.

Comets
Comets are small balls of frozen gas and dust from the cold outer edges of the Solar System. They also orbit the Sun.

Gas and ice giants

Further out, bigger planets formed from frozen substances such as water and methane, surrounded by thick layers of gas. They are the gas giants—Jupiter and Saturn—and the ice giants—Uranus and Neptune. Jupiter and Saturn formed first, about 10 million years after the Solar System began.

Jupiter
The biggest planet in the Solar System, a swirling yellowish gas giant.

Saturn
Famous for its wide orbiting rings. Jupiter, Uranus, and Neptune also have rings, but they are much fainter.

Uranus
The ice giants Uranus and Neptune formed about 90 million years into the life of the Solar System.

Neptune
Neptune is so far from the Sun that it takes more than 164 Earth years for it to complete one orbit, a Neptune "year."

THE EARLY EARTH

The Earth didn't start out as the lush blue and green planet we know today. For the first 500 million years of its existence, it had no plants, animals, or other creatures. It was a barren, lifeless world. This period is called the Hadean (meaning Hell-like) era.

Like the other planets, the Earth began as matter flying around the newly formed Sun. The matter clumped and stuck together, and the bigger the clump grew, the more powerful its gravity became, sucking in more and more material and pulling the new planet into a sphere.

The young Earth was very hot. Inside it, heavy molten iron sank down into the very center to become the core. Lighter rocky material formed the outer layer (or mantle). On the outside, rock began to cool into a solid crust. But then, just as the Earth had begun to take shape, a cataclysmic event changed the future of our planet ...

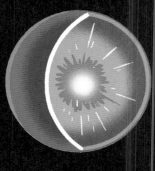 

Earth's core
Early in its life, the Earth formed separate layers inside. Iron sank to the middle, surrounded by a molten rock mantle and a hardened outer crust.

Crashhh!

A small planet called Theia, about the size of Mars, smashed into Earth 4.5 billion years ago. The energy of the impact melted and combined the two planets. A massive amount of rock flew off into space, eventually coming together to form Earth's Moon, which orbits at a distance of about 238,855 miles.

What was it like on early Earth?

Early Earth was no place for life to exist. It was hot, up to 446°F (230°C). The early atmosphere didn't block any of the Sun's powerful rays, and it contained hardly any oxygen, which animals need to breathe. Earth was also a dangerous place, with frequent impacts from the asteroids and comets that were flying around the early Solar System.

Watery world

Today, oceans cover just over 70% of the Earth's surface. Where did all this water come from? First, about 4.3 billion years ago, volcanoes poured out gases that included water vapor, and second, Earth was bombarded with many water-rich asteroids and comets. At first, Earth was so hot that the water stayed as gas, but, as the planet cooled, water began to condense into liquid, forming the first oceans.

Crust and plates

4.4 billion years ago the Earth's crust wasn't the way it is today, with continents, mountains, and soil. It was a thin layer of rock all over, with volcanic eruptions constantly breaking through it. Over millions of years the crust cooled and thickened. Hot molten rock, or magma, churned underneath it, helping to form the first tectonic plates—sections of crust that constantly shifted and reformed. These early plates were smaller than the huge tectonic plates the Earth has today.

LIFE BEGINS

Some time around 4 billion years ago, the first very small, simple life forms developed on Earth. No one knows exactly how or where this happened, and there are several theories. Some say that living cells could have reached the Earth on an asteroid or comet. But most say that a mixture of chemicals must have combined to make the first simple cells.

To work, living things need several types of chemical, including fats and sugars, and amino acids, which make proteins. These could all have formed when chemicals on Earth reacted together, helped by lightning, asteroid impacts, and the Sun's ultraviolet rays.

Life also needs water, so it probably first formed in a warm pond or mud pool where the right chemicals had become concentrated together. This life-creating mixture is sometimes called the "primordial soup."

The first cell

Cells are the basic unit of life. They have an outer skin, which surrounds a string-like chemical that can build proteins and copy itself. This is usually DNA, but in the first cells it was probably a similar, but simpler, chemical called RNA. DNA developed later, and probably replaced RNA because it's tougher and less easily damaged.

A common ancestor

All living things today are built using the same system of cells that contain DNA. Plant and animal cells are more complex than the very first cell, but they have the same basic parts and work by copying themselves. This means that all life on Earth must have developed from one early living DNA-based cell. We don't know what it was, but it's known as LUCA—the Last Universal Common Ancestor.

PLANTS

FUNGI

ANIMALS

Eukaryotes have a nucleus, or control center, and mini "organs" called organelles. They evolved into animals, plants, and fungi.

Eukaryote

About 2.7 billion years ago, early cells branched into simpler bacteria and archaea, and more complex cells called eukaryotes.

First living cells

LUCA

Bacteria and Archaea

Early evolution

Between 4 billion and 500 million years ago, as early living things copied themselves over and over again, life began to evolve. This happens because of mutations—errors that can creep in when RNA and DNA copy themselves. Over time, new life forms branched off from older ones in a tree-like pattern, creating more and more types, or species, of living thing.

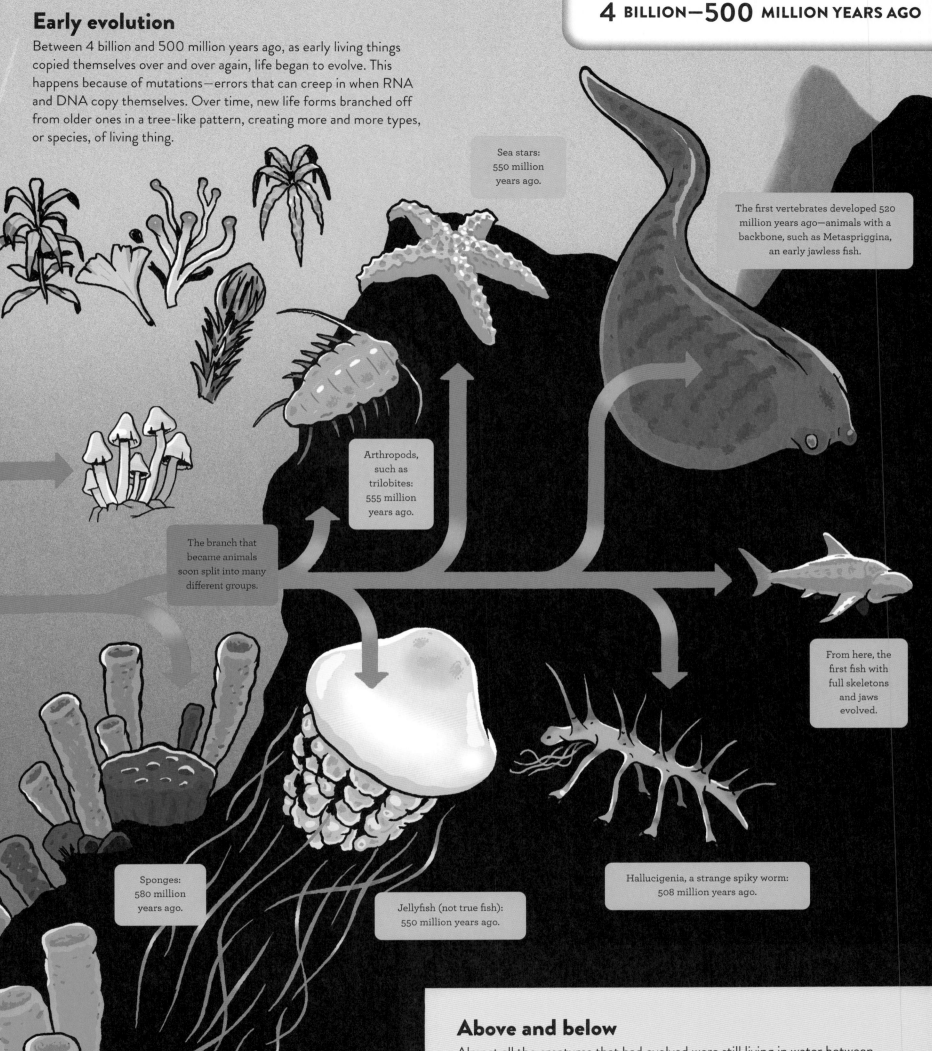

Sea stars: 550 million years ago.

The first vertebrates developed 520 million years ago—animals with a backbone, such as Metaspriggina, an early jawless fish.

Arthropods, such as trilobites: 555 million years ago.

The branch that became animals soon split into many different groups.

From here, the first fish with full skeletons and jaws evolved.

Sponges: 580 million years ago.

Jellyfish (not true fish): 550 million years ago.

Hallucigenia, a strange spiky worm: 508 million years ago.

Above and below

Almost all the creatures that had evolved were still living in water between 4 billion and 500 million years ago. Today, a layer of ozone (a type of oxygen) helps to protect us from the Sun's ultraviolet rays, but it didn't form until about 600 million years ago. After that, it became easier for living things to survive on land.

By 500 million years ago, the Earth's crust had formed continents dotted around a huge ocean. The sections of crust, called tectonic plates, slowly moved, constantly rearranging and reshaping the land. This is still happening today, but so slowly that we don't notice!

LAND INVASION

No one knows which living things were the first to make it on to land. Some ancient bacteria and mold probably washed ashore from seas or lakes, or were thrown out of geysers, and survived nearby. This could have happened billions of years ago. From about half a billion years ago a takeover began, as many more living things moved on to the land. The first plants were water plants, but plants need sunlight to grow so they had to live near the surface of the water. By 500 million years ago, early clay soil had collected on land, and it was easier for some plants to gradually move ashore, where they could get more sunlight and space to grow.

These land plants could be eaten, and they also released oxygen into the atmosphere. Both of these things paved the way for animals to populate the land.

Some plants grew bigger and bigger, and became early trees, like this cycad.

By 360 million years ago, plants like this fern were common on land.

The first land plants

500 million years ago, the first land plants were low and flat, a bit like today's moss. After about 50 million years, plants such as Cooksonia evolved to be stronger, so that they could stand upright without water to support their weight.

About 410 million years ago, some insects became the first living things to evolve flight.

The first land animals

The first land animals, about 450 million years ago, were arthropods: centipedes, millipedes, and scorpions. Their jointed legs helped them to move around out of the water, and their tough exoskeletons prevented them from drying out in the air. For millions of years insects, spiders, and other creepy-crawlies dominated the land—and some grew to enormous sizes.

Arthropleura were giant millipedes that grew to around 8 feet long.

Some tetrapods evolved into the lizard-like archosaurs, the ancestors of the dinosaurs.

Ice Age

Plants take in carbon dioxide gas and give out oxygen. When they spread on to land, this added a lot more oxygen to the Earth's atmosphere. Carbon dioxide traps heat, but oxygen doesn't. This led to the world cooling down into an Ice Age about 440 million years ago—one of the many times in its history that the Earth has cooled or warmed.

Meanwhile, in the sea ...

While some creatures took over the land, some stayed in the sea and continued to evolve. Between 500 and 250 million years ago, many amazing creatures swam in the world's waters.

Tetrapods

360 million years ago fish continued to evolve in the water, developing bony skeletons and fins. Some of them began to use their fins to "walk" around on the shallow seabeds. They evolved into a group of animals called tetrapods—meaning "four feet." At first, they probably came on to land occasionally to find food or avoid predators. Gradually, some evolved into the first amphibians, and then into

450 million years ago the first sharks evolved. Stethacanthus was a strange early shark with tooth-like scales on a tall platform on the top of its dorsal fin.

THE DINOSAUR AGE

The most famous era in prehistory was the age of the dinosaurs. It lasted about 185 million years, and more than 700 different dinosaur species lived during that time. But these well-known land reptiles weren't the only story, as reptiles also dominated the skies and the seas. This time is known as the Mesozoic era. It's divided into three main periods: Triassic (251–200 million years ago), Jurassic (200–145 mya), and Cretaceous (145–66 mya).

In the air

Near the start of the dinosaur age, some small lizard-like animals evolved wings made of flaps of skin, like a bat's. They became the pterosaurs, flying reptiles. Over time, some evolved to be much bigger.

Rhamphorhynchus
159–144 mya

Preondactylus
215–200 mya

Argentinosaurus huinculensis
The biggest dino of all: 97–93 mya

Eoraptor
237–228 mya

Spinosaurus
95–75 mya

On the land

We may think of "the age of the dinosaurs," but, of course, like other animals, different dinosaurs evolved and died out at different times, and they didn't all exist together. They also came in many sizes, and were not all enormous.

Many new plant species evolved as well. The profusion of plants provided food for the dinosaurs, helping them to thrive and grow large as time passed.

Plateosaurus
229–200 mya

In the water

Meanwhile, many types of water reptile evolved in the seas, and some of those also grew to huge sizes.

Ichthyosaur shonisaurus
232–212 mya

Plesiosaurus dolichodeirus
208–66 mya

Kronosaurus
145–100 mya

Pteranodon longiceps
85–75 mya

Quetzalcoatlus
72–66 mya

Tyrannosaurus rex
68–66 mya

Velociraptor
77–70 mya

Triceratops
68–66 mya

Albertonectes
83–70 mya

So, what happened to the dinosaurs?

About 66 million years ago, a massive asteroid hit the Earth, near what is now Mexico, causing huge tidal waves, earthquakes, and volcanic eruptions around the world. Large amounts of ash and dust darkened the sky and cooled the climate. The lack of sunlight killed plants, leading to a worldwide shortage of food. Many living things, especially larger ones, died out—an event that is now known as the KT mass extinction. They included all the dinosaurs still around at that time.

Who survived?

Earlier in the dinosaur age, bird-like dinosaurs such as Archaeopteryx had evolved into the first true birds. Some of these early birds survived the mass extinction to become the birds we know today.

Some smaller reptiles also survived, and they have evolved into today's reptiles, such as crocodiles, lizards, and snakes.

Fish, squid, and lots of other sea creatures survived, including some water reptiles.

Helped by their small size, many insects and other creepy-crawlies kept going, too.

Some small mammals were also able to survive the mass extinction. They emerged afterwards, ready to take over the world ...

RISE OF THE MAMMALS

Roughly 60 million years ago, 6 million years after the extinction of the dinosaurs, plant life recovered and started to thrive again, providing food for animals to grow.

Mammals evolved into many new and different species, taking the place of the dinosaurs. This was when a lot of the types of mammal we know today, such as cats, bats and horses, first appeared, and it is known as the Cenozoic era, or the "age of mammals."

About 55 million years ago a very different type of mammal began to develop. Their eyes moved around to the front of their faces, their snouts became smaller and their brains grew larger. They developed hand-like parts on their arms and legs, useful for climbing in trees. These were the primates, the early ancestors of human beings.

First primates
Aegyptopithecus, an early primate, first evolved 30 million years ago and could be an early ancestor of human beings.

Back to the sea
Some small, furry land mammals began living partly in water. They eventually evolved into species such as durodon. These were the first cetaceans—sea mammals such as whales and dolphins.

What are mammals?

Like dinosaurs, mammals evolved from early reptiles during the Triassic period. While reptiles had scaly skin and, later on, feathers, mammals evolved to be furry. They are also warm-blooded, meaning they can keep their body temperature warmer than their surroundings; and mother mammals feed their babies with milk.

Carnivores
Some early mammals evolved into weasel-like hunters. They were the ancestors of carnivores such as dogs, cats, and bears. Hesperocyon was one of the first dogs, 36 million years ago.

Monster mammals

About 60 million years ago a major group of mammals appeared: the ungulates, or hoofed mammals. They were mainly plant-eaters, and many of them grew huge.

Megacerops: 16 feet long
This creature had two rounded horns on its nose, similar to some rhinos today.

Paraceratherium: 25 feet long
A ginormous long-necked animal, like a cross between a rhino and a giraffe.

Andrewsarchus: 10–13 feet long
This was a big meat-eater with a huge head and jaws.

Entelodont: 10 feet long
Also called "terminator pigs," these were giant pig-like beasts.

Flying mammals
When bats, such as Icaronycteris, first evolved about 53 million years ago, they became the only mammals that can truly fly. It was the fourth time flight had evolved in Earth's history—after insects, pterosaurs, and birds.

Mini mammals
Small, fast-moving rodents such as Ischyromys evolved soon after the KT mass extinction. Even ancient rodents look very similar to modern ones such as rats and squirrels.

Age of the flowers

The KT mass extinction wiped out many plant species. As they recovered, new flowering plants and trees evolved and began to dominate the Earth. All of these extra flowers, fruit, seeds, and pollen meant more food for insects and birds, helping them to flourish, too. Some plants began to rely on insects or bats to pollinate them.

THE FIRST HUMANS

Somewhere between 6 and 4 million years ago, the first human-like animals developed. They were a type of ape, part of the primate family of mammals. Humans would go on to dominate the world—but it took many stages for our species to evolve into the humans of today.

There were several species of early human in the past. Humans did not evolve from chimps, as some people think. Instead, humans and the other apes all evolved separately, from much earlier ancestors. Homo sapiens—the humans of today—first appeared between 300,000 and 200,000 years ago. There were actually several different species of human until, about 30,000 years ago, we became the last remaining humans.

Human features

As humans evolved, between 6 million and 200,000 years ago, a number of changes happened that made us very different from most other animals. The illustration below shows what these were.

Brain became bigger and more complex.

Jaw and teeth became smaller and weaker.

Most thick body hair was lost.

Hands became more skilled and better at fine, careful movements.

Humans spent less time in trees and moved mainly on to the ground, evolving to walk upright.

Family tree

No one knows exactly how all the ape species were related, but this tree shows one possibility.

Early ancestor

Orangutan

Gorilla

Chimpanzee

Australopithecus ("Southern ape")

Paranthropus ("Alongside humans")

Homo habilis ("Handy human")

Homo floresiensis ("Flores human")

Homo erectus ("Upright human")

Homo denisova ("Denisova human")

Homo neanderthalensis ("Neander Valley human")

Homo sapiens ("Smart human")

Spreading across the world

Fossils show that the first humans evolved in eastern Africa and began spreading out into Europe and Asia about 2 million years ago, and into the Americas across a land bridge from the far east of Russia. By 12,000 years ago, modern humans had reached most parts of the planet.

Stone Age life

Stone Age people lived in caves, but also made shelters from stones, branches, or animal skins to keep warm, since they were now mostly hairless. Their ability to create fire kept them warm and safe and allowed them to cook their food. They hunted in groups for large animals such as buffalo for their meat and skins.

> By 15,000 years ago, people were living with pet dogs, bred from tamed wild wolves.

> Women and children were more likely to gather plant food than to hunt.

Human habits

Until about 12,000 years ago, humans probably lived in smallish groups, hunting and fishing for food, and collecting plant food such as nuts, mushrooms, and berries. Their big brains and hardworking hands helped them to make tools and other inventions, as well as communicate in spoken language, and create art and music.

17,000 years ago
Lascaux

Paintings of people and animals, found in the Lascaux cave, France.

Art history

Prehistoric art has been found all over the world, dating far back into the Stone Age.

75,000 years ago
Blombos beads

Shells made into beads, maybe for making a necklace, from the Blombos Cave in South Africa.

40,000 years ago
Lion-man

A human with a lion's head, carved from a mammoth tusk, found in a cave in Germany.

SETTLING DOWN

For hundreds of thousands of years early humans lived in small, nomadic groups. Then, about 12,000 years ago, as the most recent Ice Age came to an end, that all began to change.

People started growing plants for food, and keeping their own herds of animals instead of having to chase them across the countryside. It turned out to be an easier and much more reliable way to get enough to eat, and so many humans settled down in permanent villages.

Humans thrived on this new farming lifestyle. They were able to have more children and they had more time to develop other things: crafts such as pottery, and inventions and discoveries such as metalwork and weaving.

Farming catches on

Farming began in warm climates with plenty of sunshine and rain, especially a part of the Middle East known as the Fertile Crescent, and the Yellow and Yangtze river valleys in China. Gradually, it spread to the rest of the world.

1. Fertile Crescent: Barley
2. Yangtze River: Rice
3. Yellow River: Millet
4. South America: Potatoes
5. Africa: Sorghum
6. New Guinea: Taro

Village life

The first human settlements were usually close to a river or spring to provide water, and surrounded by crop-growing and animal-herding areas. About 9,400 years ago, for example, people lived in villages like this one in Turkey, known as Çatalhöyük, which is still standing today!

Çatalhöyük was built on a hill overlooking a plain.

People ground up grains into flour, made dough and cooked a type of simple flatbread.

Trade and money

Early people had been trading for thousands of years, by swapping useful items with one another. About 9,000 years ago, as farming developed, people began to use livestock such as cattle and goats, and grain such as barley, as the first forms of money.

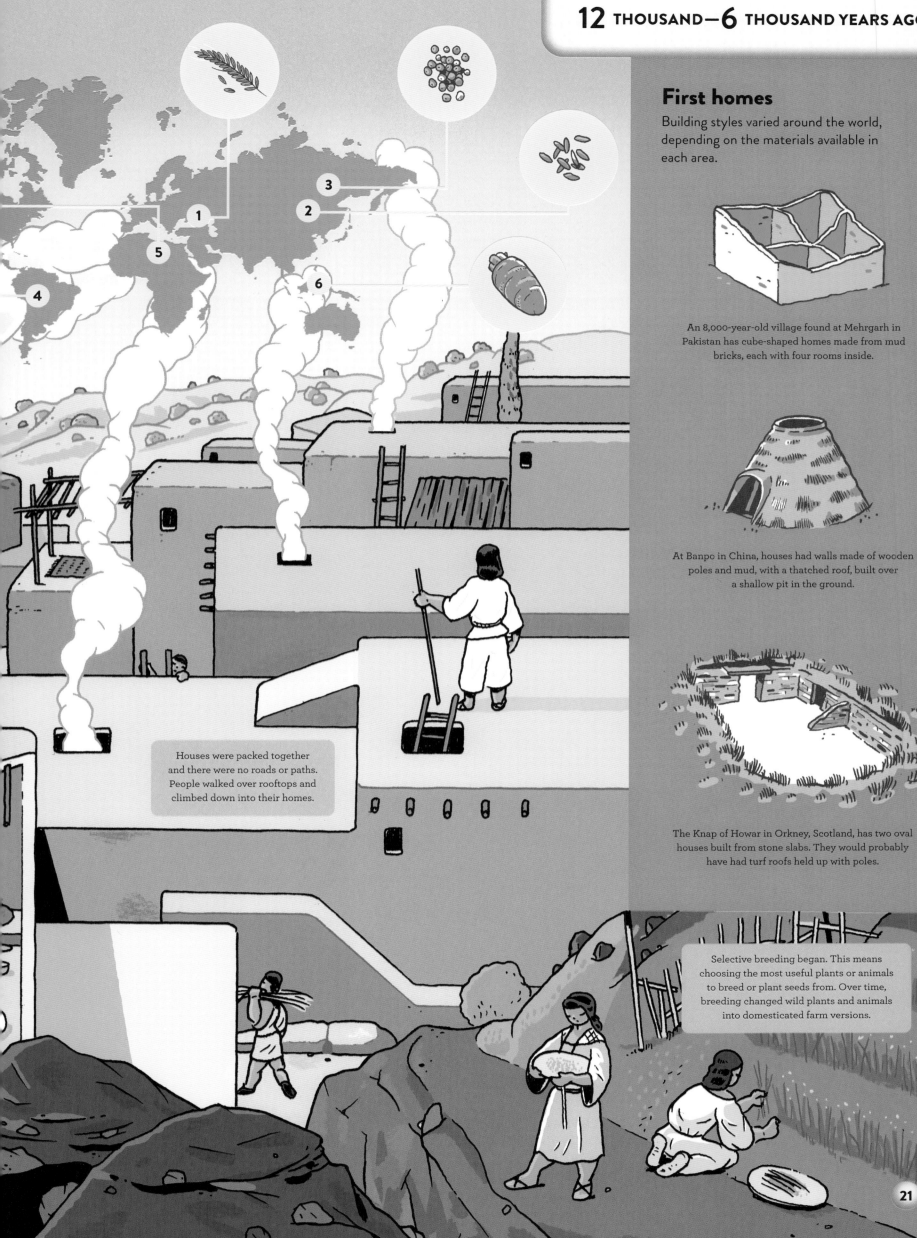

First homes

Building styles varied around the world, depending on the materials available in each area.

An 8,000-year-old village found at Mehrgarh in Pakistan has cube-shaped homes made from mud bricks, each with four rooms inside.

At Banpo in China, houses had walls made of wooden poles and mud, with a thatched roof, built over a shallow pit in the ground.

The Knap of Howar in Orkney, Scotland, has two oval houses built from stone slabs. They would probably have had turf roofs held up with poles.

Houses were packed together and there were no roads or paths. People walked over rooftops and climbed down into their homes.

Selective breeding began. This means choosing the most useful plants or animals to breed or plant seeds from. Over time, breeding changed wild plants and animals into domesticated farm versions.

CITIES, CIVILIZATIONS, AND EMPIRES

From about 6,000 years ago, early societies in some parts of the world became more advanced and complex. They built the first cities, and began to have kings and queens, armies, and the first writing systems.

The earliest cities were probably in Sumer in ancient Mesopotamia (modern-day Iraq and Kuwait), one of the areas where farming began. Sumer's cities included Uruk, Ur, and Eridu. At the heart of these cities were large buildings such as temples and palaces, which were surrounded by smaller homes, then farmland.

The Ziggurat of Ur, a kind of Sumerian temple.

A royal palace and tombs were central to the city.

Part of the Sumerian city of Ur, in around 2,000 BCE.

Surrounding walls protected the city from invaders.

World-changing inventions

This was an age of all kinds of important inventions, and many of them are still around today.

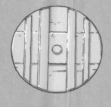

The wheel, first used in Sumer in about 3,500 BCE, was one of the most useful inventions ever.

People probably began using the beans of the cocoa tree to make chocolate drinks in what is now Mexico, about 2,000 BCE.

The first coins are thought to have been made in Lydia, in what is now Turkey, in about 600 BCE.

The first paper appeared in 100 CE in China, and was made from fibers of cloth and bark.

History starts here!

Of course, Earth already had a long history. But, strictly speaking, history means records that are written down—and for that, you need writing. Writing began in Sumer about 5,500 years ago (in 3,500 BCE), but was also invented separately in other places. The earliest writing systems used small symbols and pictures to stand for words.

Sun

Early Sumerian cuneiform
3,500 BCE

Water

Ancient Egyptian hieroglyphs
3,300 BCE

Rain

Shang oracle bone script
1,250 BCE

Houses and workshops were made from mudbricks and mud plaster.

Power and control

Cities and their leaders often controlled large surrounding areas, and a big city needed a powerful ruler, so the first kings and queens also date from this time. About 4,300 years ago (in 2,300 BCE), King Sargon of Akkad became one of the first leaders to keep a full-time trained army. He used it to conquer a large area, including other cities, which became the Akkadian empire. More empires formed around the world, growing, shrinking, or being taken over at different times.

Ancient Egypt

3100 BCE to 500 BCE
In North Africa, close to Sumer, Egypt became a complex ancient empire. It had many cities, and its people were advanced in building, medicine, writing, and exploration by sea.

The Minoans

2700 BCE to 1100 BCE
The mysterious Minoans, who lived on the island of Crete, dominated the Mediterranean before the age of ancient Greece. They were brilliant sailors, and they are thought to have practiced the ritual of bull-leaping.

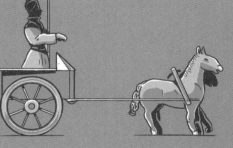

Shang dynasty

1600 BCE to 1046 BCE
The Shang is the oldest known Chinese dynasty, ruling a large area of eastern China. They developed incredible bronzework, war chariots, calendars, and writing systems.

The Olmec

1500 BCE to 400 BCE
The Olmec civilization was in present-day Mexico. The name Olmec means "rubber people"—they extracted rubber from the rubber tree, and traded it with other peoples. They're also known for their carved sculptures.

Ancient Rome

800 BCE to 500 CE
This hugely powerful empire was centered on Rome, now in Italy, but took over large areas of Africa, the Middle East, and Europe. It's famous for its amazing buildings, complex military, and great writers and artists.

SCIENCE, ART, AND DISCOVERY

Over the next 1,000 years, people around the world studied, experimented, created, and explored, leading to a transformation of science, art, and culture.

From the 1200s to the 1500s, traders, explorers, and adventurers began to make much longer journeys, searching for new trade routes, discovering new lands, or just exploring far and wide. Human groups who had spread across the world thousands of years earlier began to contact one another for the first time.

Voyages of discovery

1271–95: The Venetian merchant Marco Polo went on a 24-year adventure around Asia, and later wrote about his travels.

1325–54: The Moroccan scholar Ibn Battuta explored the Islamic world, and visited Europe, Asia, and Africa.

1405–33: The Chinese diplomat Zheng He led seven great voyages of exploration westwards around Asia and as far as Africa.

1519–22: The Portuguese explorer Ferdinand Magellan captained the first round-the-world voyage (although he himself died halfway through).

Islam's Golden Age
700s to 1200s

Learning flourished as Islamic scholars wrote books on medicine, surgery, chemistry, and algebra. Astronomers studied the Sun, the Moon, the planets, and the stars, and mathematicians developed the system of Arabic numerals that is still used across the modern world.

China's Science Revolution
600s to 1400s

In China, the Tang and Song dynasties encouraged science, technology, and the exchange of ideas. The Chinese invented fireworks in the 600s, and by the 900s they were using smallpox scabs to make an early kind of vaccine against the disease.

Great explorations

Around the year 1000, the Icelandic explorer Leif Erikson sailed to the coast of what is now Canada, becoming the first European to discover North America. But life in the Americas changed forever when the Italian explorer Christopher Columbus made several trips west across the Atlantic Ocean between 1492 and 1502, starting a trend of European invasion and settlement in the Americas, which became known as the New World.

The slave trade

From ancient times, people in some societies used other humans as slaves. As trade and exploration grew in the 1500s, some European nations took over land in the Americas and began shipping people from Africa to use as slaves there, mainly working on farms or plantations. Slavery was not abolished until the 1800s. Descendants of African slaves now live throughout the Americas.

Art and architecture

537: Byzantine Emperor Justinian I built the beautiful domed Hagia Sophia church. The minarets were added in the fifteenth century.

1000s: The Bayeux Tapestry depicted the conquest of England by William of Normandy, France.

1100s to 1400s: West Africa's Yoruba culture perfected bronze casting, creating detailed sculptures and masks.

1200s to 1500s: The people of Easter Island in the South Pacific made huge stone figures called *moai*.

Europe's Renaissance
1300s to 1600s

In the 1300s a revolution in science, art, and culture began in Italy and spread across Europe. The printing press was developed in the 1440s, speeding up book-printing and allowing the rapid spread of information. By the early 1600s telescopes had been invented, allowing astronomers to realize that the planets orbited the Sun, and around this time new theaters were built, William Shakespeare wrote his plays, and a new age of drama dawned.

INDUSTRIAL REVOLUTION

Throughout the 1700s and into the 1800s, a major change happened. It began in Britain, but spread quickly across Europe and America, and later around the world. Known as the Industrial Revolution, it changed the way products were made. It had a huge effect on the way people lived, worked, moved around, and spent money. In fact, it paved the way for the modern world.

Before this time, most people lived in towns or villages. They worked on farms or made products such as cloth, shoes, or pottery in their homes or in local workshops. With the invention of steam power and manufacturing machines, business owners began building factories in cities, powered at first by water wheels and then by steam engines. Cities grew as people moved there from the countryside to work in textile factories, glassworks, ironworks, and potteries.

Full steam ahead

The Industrial Revolution began with several new inventions, one of which was the steam engine. The first steam-powered boats and ships appeared in the late 1700s. In 1803 Richard Trevithick built a steam locomotive that ran on tracks, and this developed into long-distance railways.

New, stronger roads and bridges were built to carry raw materials and products into and out of the cities.

Goods were carried between countries by sea, using the new steam-powered boats and ships.

Poor air quality

The Industrial Revolution was powered mainly by burning coal. As much more coal was burned, cities became polluted with smoke and soot. It affected people's health and blackened walls and tree trunks.

Factories employed people for long hours, usually six days a week. Workers included children, and the machines were often dangerous.

Cities grew so fast that there wasn't enough space for everyone. Workers rented small, cramped homes and lived in overcrowded, dirty conditions.

Lighting up

In about 1806 the first street lighting using coal gas was installed in Rhode Island, USA. Scientists also learned to harness electricity. Alessandro Volta invented the battery in 1800, and soon afterwards Humphry Davy demonstrated an early electric light.

Buying power

The rise of manufacturing meant that there were more products for sale. Owning more possessions and keeping up with fashion wasn't only for the super-rich any more, and businesses responded by advertising in newspapers and on billboards.

School for everyone

As printing technology improved, more newspapers and books were published. More businesses and factories meant there were more jobs for people who could read, write, and count, and governments began to provide free schooling.

TECHNOLOGY

The Industrial Revolution, and the discovery of how to use electricity, led to a new wave of invention and exploration. This would revolutionize the world, making all kinds of things quicker and faster: everyday tasks, storing information, communicating over long distances, and getting from A to B.

Throughout the 1800s and early 1900s, inventors experimented with electricity and circuits, and came up with many types of new electrical technology, from light bulbs to televisions. By the mid-1900s they had also developed electronics: using the flow of electrons around circuits to control signals and carry information. This led to the development of the first computers.

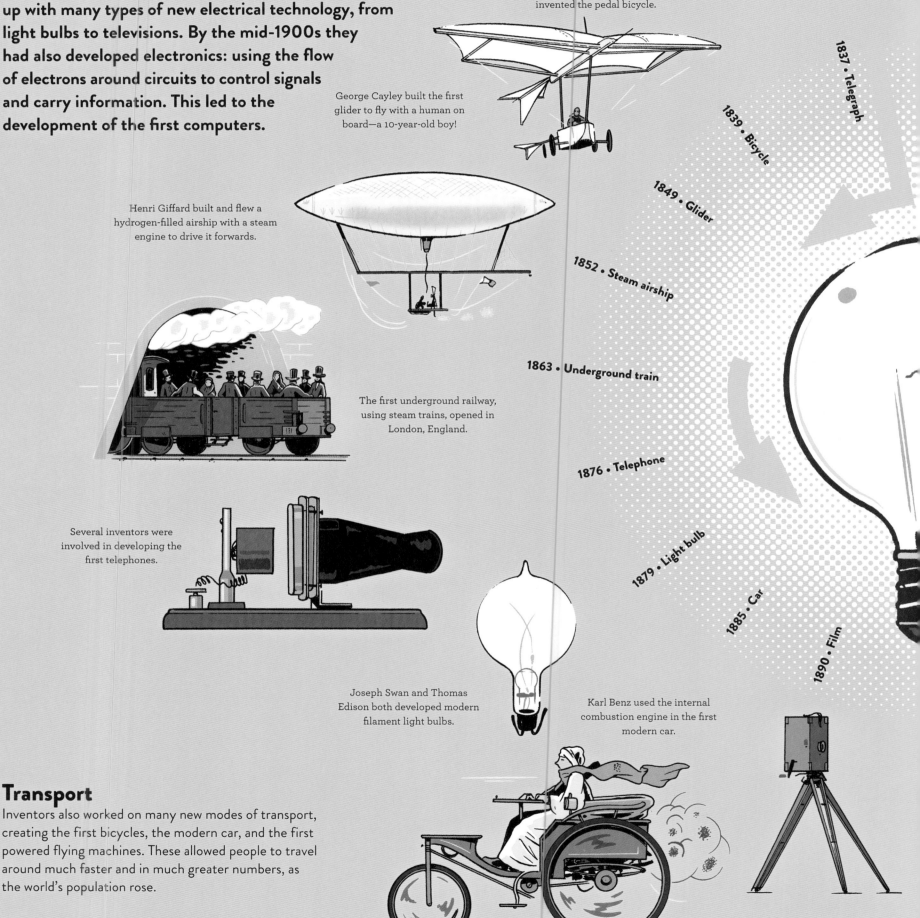

Samuel Morse, Alfred Vail, and Joseph Henry demonstrated their telegraph system, using long and short signals (dots and dashes), known as Morse code, to represent letters.

Kirkpatrick Macmillan invented the pedal bicycle.

George Cayley built the first glider to fly with a human on board—a 10-year-old boy!

Henri Giffard built and flew a hydrogen-filled airship with a steam engine to drive it forwards.

The first underground railway, using steam trains, opened in London, England.

Several inventors were involved in developing the first telephones.

Joseph Swan and Thomas Edison both developed modern filament light bulbs.

Karl Benz used the internal combustion engine in the first modern car.

1837 • Telegraph
1839 • Bicycle
1849 • Glider
1852 • Steam airship
1863 • Underground train
1876 • Telephone
1879 • Light bulb
1885 • Car
1890 • Film

Transport

Inventors also worked on many new modes of transport, creating the first bicycles, the modern car, and the first powered flying machines. These allowed people to travel around much faster and in much greater numbers, as the world's population rose.

Invention of a film camera that could shoot a series of frames to make a moving image.

Percy Spencer discovered that electromagnetic waves could be used to heat and cook food.

Igor Sikorsky flew the first modern helicopter with a single rotor and a tailplane.

Konrad Zuse's Z1 was the first programmable electric computer.

The airman Frank Whittle invented the jet engine, which would make planes faster.

Robert Goddard launched a high-speed, liquid-powered rocket that would pave the way for space flight.

1945 • Microwave oven

1939 • Helicopter power

1938 • Programmable computer

1930 • Jet engine

1926 • Modern rocket

1924 • Television

1903 • Powered heavier-than-air flight

1900 • Radio

The world at war

In the first half of the twentieth century two great wars shook the globe, and also brought more rapid developments in technology.

First World War, 1914–18

World War I began as a conflict between the European countries of Serbia and Austria-Hungary, but many other countries took sides. The newly invented airplane was adapted for use in war and the first fighter planes flew.

Second World War, 1939–45

World War II was triggered by the German leader Adolf Hitler's attempts to take over other parts of Europe. It involved many countries worldwide and ended with the detonation of nuclear bombs at Hiroshima and Nagasaki in Japan.

John Logie Baird transmitted moving images and sound using radio waves for the first time.

After the discovery of radio waves, they were used to transmit coded messages, and then sounds in 1900.

Brothers Orville and Wilbur Wright built and flew the first successful engine-powered plane.

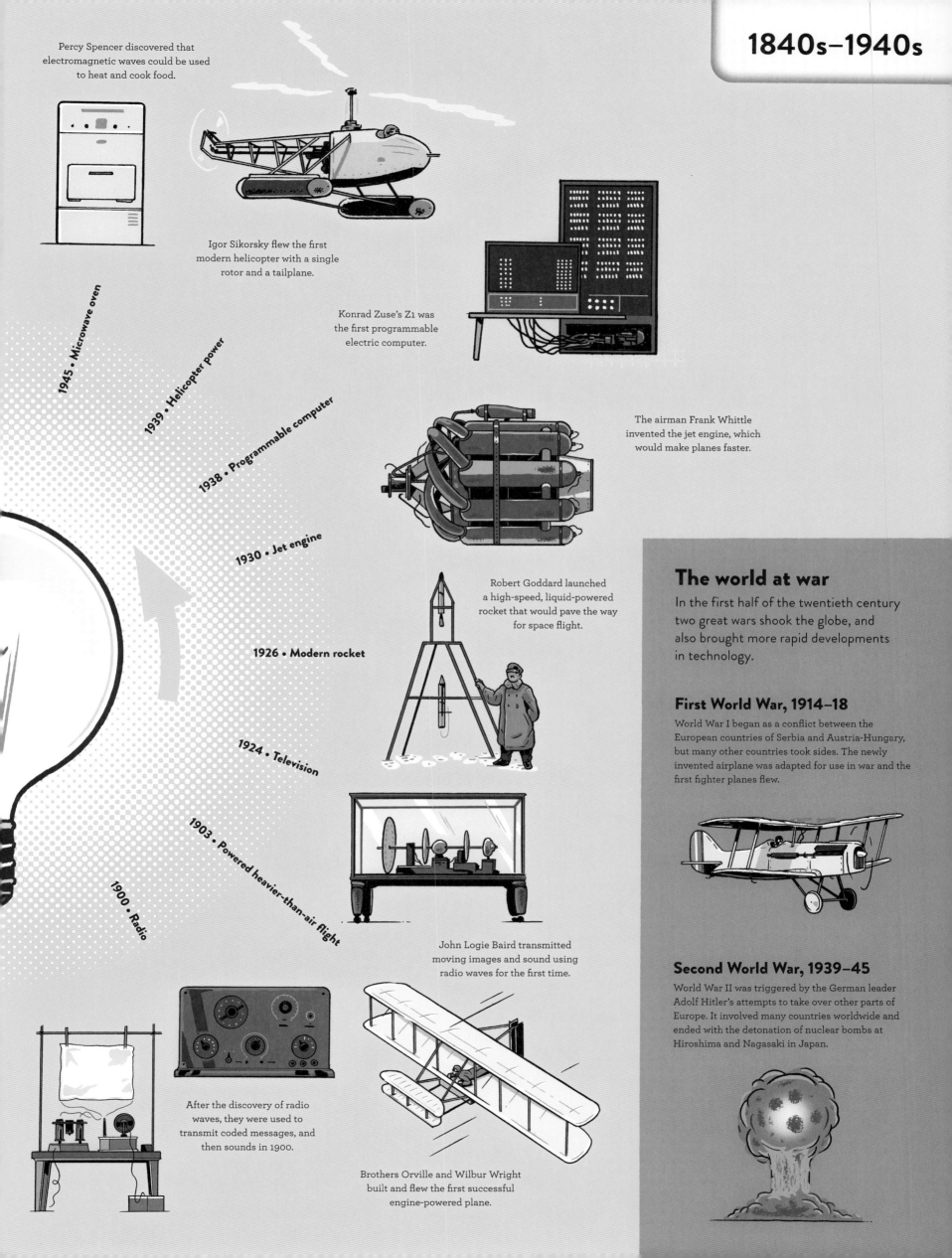

THE MODERN AGE

From the 1940s onward, technology continued to develop amazingly quickly. Scientific progress gave us modern medicines, robots, radio telescopes, and electron microscopes. In 1953 James Watson, Francis Crick, and Rosalind Franklin solved the puzzle of how DNA encodes information to make life itself work, and in 1969 humans set foot on the Moon. Today we live in a computerized world, surrounded by modern gadgets, and our electronic communications systems and satellites can reach, scan, and measure every part of the Earth.

Electronics have advanced at high speed, and computer technology has become smaller, more powerful, and more available. In the 1960s computer scientists began developing ways to network computers together to share information and messages. These early networks developed into the internet and the World Wide Web, which came into widespread use in the 1990s.

The space race

The space race was a period of space exploration related to the Cold War, when the USA and the USSR (as Russia's empire was then known) competed to launch the first satellites and crewed spacecraft. It culminated in the US astronauts Neil Armstrong and Buzz Aldrin becoming the first humans to walk on the Moon, in July 1969.

In the 1970s a new era of co-operation began, with many nations collaborating on space missions. Starting in 1998, many nations have worked together to construct and crew the International Space Station (ISS), the largest artificial satellite orbiting the Earth.

Population explosion
1945–present

The Earth's human population has been growing since prehistoric times, but it has grown fastest of all since 1945, reaching almost 8 billion in 2019. The growth rate has now slowed, and the population may start to fall again during the twenty-first century.

A connected world

Among many other changes, the internet and the web allowed online shopping and gaming, and the rise of social media, allowing users to share messages and images with a large audience. Smartphones, which were launched in the early 2000s, allowed people to carry a mini internet-linked computer around with them and access the web at any time.

Carbon dioxide in the atmosphere traps and reflects heat energy from the Sun.

Saving our planet

In the 1960s an environmental movement began as more and more people became aware of the various ways human activity was causing damage to the Earth and its wildlife. Using land for farms, cities, and roads destroyed vast areas of natural habitat, and too much fishing and hunting caused some species to die out or become endangered. Waste from factories, power stations, farms, vehicles, and packaging polluted water, land, and air, and some polluting gases—such as carbon dioxide and methane—changed the Earth's atmosphere, making it trap the Sun's heat and increase average temperatures. This change in temperature has led to the beginning of changes in climate patterns around the world.

Today, nations and individuals are trying to reduce greenhouse gas emissions, change transport methods, and replace fuel-burning energy sources with renewables such as wind and solar power, in an attempt to limit global warming and prevent harm to the planet.

INDEX

Published in 2020
by Laurence King Publishing
361–373 City Road
London EC1V 1LR
United Kingdom
T +44 20 7841 6900
enquiries@laurenceking.com
www.laurenceking.com

Illustrations © 2020 Jan Van Der Veken
Text © 2020 Anna Claybourne

A catalog record for this book is
available from the British Library.

ISBN: 978 1 78627 684 1

Printed in the Netherlands

Laurence King Publishing is committed
to ethical and sustainable production.
We are proud participants in The Book
Chain Project.® bookchainproject.com